Rise, Reset, and Recover

Emotional Recharge for The Souls

Valerie Jones

Introduction

Welcome Letter from the Author

Dear Reader,

If you've picked up this book, chances are you're searching for something. Perhaps it's clarity, comfort, or simply a way forward through an emotional storm. Whatever has brought you here, I want you to know that you are not alone.

Life has a way of throwing unexpected challenges our way. These challenges often leave us feeling lost, overwhelmed, or even broken. We all experience moments of doubt, pain, and uncertainty, but within each of us lies an inner compass. A compass that, when understood and nurtured, can guide us toward healing and resilience.

The Healing Compass was born out of a deep desire to help others navigate their emotional journeys with greater awareness, self-compassion, and strength. This book is not about quick fixes or pretending pain doesn't exist. Instead, it offers tools, insights, and real-life strategies to help you move through your struggles with clarity and purpose.

My hope is that as you turn these pages, you'll find not only guidance but also a sense of connection. Healing is not a straight path—it is a journey of self-discovery, one that requires patience and courage. But with the right mindset and resources, it is possible to emerge stronger, wiser, and more in tune with yourself.

I have also added a fun little activity for you to do at the end of each chapter. These activities can help you get through minor stuff. Note that these are not from a professional perspective. If you are in need of professional help, please contact your nearest mental health institute.

So take a deep breath. You are exactly where you need to be. Let's embark on this journey together.

With warmth and understanding,

Valerie Jones

How to Get the Most Out of This Book

Imagine you're setting out on a journey, one that promises clarity, healing, and a deeper understanding of yourself. You wouldn't begin without a map or a compass, and you certainly wouldn't expect to reach your destination in a single day. Healing is much the same. It's a process, not a quick fix. And like any journey, how you navigate it will determine what you take away from the experience.

As you read this book, I encourage you to approach it with an open heart and a curious mind. Some lessons may resonate instantly, while others might challenge you. That's okay. Growth often comes in layers. It reveals itself over time. If something sparks a realization or tugs at something deep inside you, pause. Reflect. Let the words settle before moving on.

Think of this book as a conversation, not just a collection of pages. Engage with it. Underline passages that speak to you, jot down thoughts in the margins, and take a moment to truly absorb each idea before rushing to the next. Healing isn't about speed; it's about understanding. Sometimes, the most powerful insights come when you simply sit with them.

In a world that moves at an exhausting pace, it's easy to fall into the habit of rushing. People rush through work, through conversations, through life itself. But healing is not something that can be hurried. It requires time, patience, and a willingness to sit with your thoughts rather than sprint past them.

While reading each chapter, resist the urge to treat it as just another thing to check off your to-do list. This isn't about consuming information as quickly as possible; it's about internalizing it, making it a part of you. Each chapter is meant to be a stepping stone, not just a page to flip through.

One of the most effective ways to engage with these insights is through journaling. Writing down your thoughts allows you to process them in a way that simply reading cannot. It helps you track your progress, recognize patterns in your emotions, and create a deeper sense of self-awareness. You don't need to write pages. Sometimes, a few sentences are enough to bring clarity.

And don't be afraid to revisit chapters. Healing is not linear, and the lessons you take away today may look different when you return to them weeks or months from now. What might not seem relevant at one point in your life could suddenly become the exact wisdom you need later. Growth happens in layers, and sometimes, the most profound realizations come when we least expect them.

So, as you move through this book, permit yourself to slow down. Take breaks when you need to. Sit with the discomfort, celebrate the breakthroughs, and allow each chapter to guide you at its own pace.

Along the way, you'll find exercises and reflections designed to help you put these ideas into practice. I encourage you to participate actively. It's one thing to read about healing; it's another to experience it. Small, intentional changes often lead to the biggest transformations.

Reading about healing is one thing, and experiencing it is another. Knowledge is powerful, but real transformation happens when you put what you learn into action. That's why, throughout this book, you'll find exercises designed to help you apply the concepts in a tangible way.

And don't go on this journey alone. Share your thoughts with a friend, discuss insights that resonate with you, and be open to the wisdom that others bring into your life. Healing becomes even more powerful when we allow ourselves to connect.

Most importantly, be kind to yourself. There's no "right" way to heal, no perfect path to follow. Some days will feel lighter than others, and that's part of the process. What matters is that you keep moving forward, step by step, at your own pace.

Take a deep breath, trust the process, and let's begin this journey together.

Table of Contents

Chapter 1:
Emotional Storms and the Compass Framework

Life is full of ups and downs, moments of joy, and moments of struggle. But sometimes, we experience something deeper. One can describe it as an emotional storm. These storms are not just bad moods or temporary stress; they are intense waves of emotion that shake us to our core. They can come in many forms: heartbreak, grief, betrayal, overwhelming anxiety, or the sudden realization that life isn't going the way we had hoped.

An emotional storm doesn't just affect how we feel—it influences how we think, how we make decisions, and how we see the world. When caught in one, everything can seem distorted. A minor setback may feel like a catastrophe. Hope can seem distant, and even the simplest tasks may feel impossible. Just as a real storm can turn a familiar landscape into an unfamiliar and chaotic scene, an emotional storm can make life feel unpredictable and overwhelming.

But here's the truth: storms, no matter how fierce, do not last forever. They pass. And just as nature rebuilds itself after a storm, we too have the ability to heal, to grow, and to find clarity once again. The key is learning how to navigate through them rather than letting them consume us.

Emotional storms are part of the natural life. Events, both big and small, trigger them and shake us, sometimes suddenly, sometimes gradually. It's important to realize that they don't appear out of nowhere. Often, they are the result of accumulated emotions, pressures, or unmet needs that have nowhere else to go but to break free in an explosive way.

For instance, when we experience a loss, whether it's the end of a relationship, the death of someone close to us, or even the loss of a dream. It can send shockwaves through our emotional system. Or sometimes, it's the slow, steady buildup of stress and worry. Maybe it's the constant juggle of work, family, and personal expectations, and eventually, it just becomes too much to hold in. That's when the storm brews, often catching us off guard.

There are also times when the storm hits without a clear trigger. It can be the weight of suppressed emotions from the past or the pressure of societal expectations weighing heavily on our shoulders. Life doesn't always unfold in a straight line. The curveballs it throws at us don't always make sense. And sometimes, these emotional storms are what happens when our inner world collides with the unpredictability of the external world.

But here's the most important part: these storms are not something to fear or avoid. They are part of our human experience. They're our mind and body's way of processing the emotions that come with life's challenges. Understanding why they happen can help us take a step back, breathe, and realize that they are not a sign of weakness or failure. They are a natural response to life's difficulties.

When we're caught in the midst of an emotional storm, everything feels affected—our thoughts, our relationships, our bodies. It's like we're suddenly out of sync with ourselves and the world around us. Every part of our life feels touched by the storm in some way, sometimes in ways we don't even notice right away.

Take, for example, our mental and emotional health. When an emotional storm strikes, it's easy to feel like our thoughts are clouded or disconnected from reality. We might feel anxious, uncertain, or even lost in our own emotions. The very foundation of our mental state becomes shaky, and simple decisions that would usually be easy become overwhelming. In these moments, it's hard to see clearly, and sometimes it feels like we're drowning in our own thoughts.

Our relationships can feel the impact, too. During an emotional storm, we may withdraw from those we care about or lash out at them in frustration. We might find it hard to communicate what we're going through or fear that others won't understand. Sometimes, we unintentionally push people away, not because we want to, but because the storm inside us has made it difficult to connect. It's easy to isolate ourselves, but this only deepens the sense of loneliness and confusion.

At work, our productivity often takes a hit. When emotions are running high, it can feel impossible to focus. What was once a straightforward task can suddenly feel monumental, and the pressure to perform can create even more stress. This often leads to a vicious cycle of guilt, as we feel we should be doing better but can't seem to pull ourselves together.

Even our physical health isn't immune to the effects of emotional storms. When we're under stress, our bodies react. We might notice tension in our muscles, headaches, or even digestive issues. The storm doesn't just exist in our minds. It manifests physically, draining our energy and making it harder to function. The emotional weight can feel like it's dragging us down, both mentally and physically.

And perhaps most notably, an emotional storm can disrupt our self-perception. When we're in the thick of it, it's easy to forget who we are outside of our emotions. We may start to identify ourselves as "broken" or "too much" or believe that we aren't strong enough to handle the challenges we're facing. But the storm doesn't define us. It's simply a part of the journey. Our true strength lies in how we rise above it.

Now that we've explored how emotional storms impact us, it's time to talk about how we can weather them. Because, though they may feel overwhelming, they don't have to define us.

The first step in weathering any emotional storm is to acknowledge it. Denial only prolongs the intensity. When a storm hits, allow yourself to feel it. Don't try to push your emotions away or pretend they aren't there. It's okay not to have everything together right away. Give yourself permission to feel the full weight of your emotions, whether it's grief, anger, or confusion. Acceptance is the first step toward healing.

Next, center yourself. When the storm feels like it's sweeping you away, pause and take a deep breath. Simple breathing exercises can calm your nervous system and bring you back into the present moment. Focus on the rhythm of your breath and let each inhale and exhale ground you. This is your moment to regain some control, to remind yourself that you can weather this.

It's also important to reach out for support. You don't have to go through it alone. Talking to someone can provide comfort and perspective. This someone can be a friend, a family member, or a therapist. Sometimes, just voicing your thoughts can lift the burden. There's no shame in asking for help; in fact, it's one of the most powerful ways to navigate through a storm.

Shift your focus to things that nurture your soul. Self-care becomes especially important during emotional storms. Whether it's going for a walk, taking a bath, or listening to music that soothes you, find small ways to take care of your body and mind. Engaging in activities that bring you peace can act as an anchor. It prevents you from being swept away by the storm's intensity.

During the storm, it can also help to reframe the situation. Storms are not only challenges; they are opportunities to grow. Look for the lessons within your struggle. What can you learn from this experience? What is it teaching you about yourself, your boundaries, or your needs? Reframing the storm as a chance for growth shifts your perspective from victimhood to empowerment.

And finally, practice patience. Healing takes time. Emotional storms don't dissipate overnight, and neither do their effects. Be patient with yourself. Recognize that just like a storm eventually clears, so too will your emotional turmoil. Trust in your ability to recover, and trust in the process of healing. You will emerge from this stronger, more grounded, and more resilient.

Remember, emotional storms may come, but they do not last forever. By learning to weather them with awareness, patience, and compassion, we can rise above the chaos and emerge with greater clarity and strength.

Now that we've explored the nature of emotional storms and their impact on our lives, it's time to introduce a method that can help guide us through these challenging moments with clarity and resilience: the RPNB method: Reflect, Pause, Navigate, and Balance.

Navigating through emotional storms requires more than just enduring the storm itself. It's about understanding how to move through it with intention and self-awareness. The RPNB method is designed to guide you through this journey, offering a structured approach to help you weather the storm and emerge stronger on the other side. These four compass points—Reflect, Pause, Navigate, and Balance—serve as essential tools to help you regain clarity, focus, and inner peace during emotional upheaval.

The first compass point, **Pause**, is all about taking a moment to stop, breathe, and create space. When caught in the emotional whirlwind, it's easy to feel swept away by the intensity of your feelings, acting impulsively or making decisions that may not serve you in the long run. Pausing is about giving yourself permission to step back and allow your emotions to settle, even if just for a few moments. This act of stillness helps you break the automatic response to your emotions. It creates a small window of clarity where you can assess the situation without being completely overwhelmed by it.

Think of **Pause** as the calm before the storm's full impact. When you pause, you allow yourself to take a breath, giving your mind and body the chance to center themselves before rushing into reactions. This simple yet powerful step helps you become more mindful of your emotional state, setting the tone for the rest of your journey through the storm.

Once you've taken a moment to pause, it's time to **Reflect**. Reflection is about diving deeper into your emotional experience, examining what's really going on beneath the surface. What triggered the storm? What underlying thoughts or beliefs are fueling your emotions? By reflecting on your feelings, you can begin to uncover patterns and gain insight into the root causes of the turmoil.

Reflection doesn't mean overanalyzing or getting stuck in your emotions; it's about becoming more aware of your inner landscape. Ask yourself questions like:

What am I really feeling right now?

Where is this feeling coming from?

Is there a past experience influencing my reaction?

This process allows you to take ownership of your emotions, giving you a greater understanding of yourself and your responses. Reflection creates an opportunity to break free from automatic reactions, enabling you to approach the storm with a deeper sense of awareness and control.

Once you've paused and reflected, it's time to **Navigate**. This compass point is about moving forward with intention. It's not about ignoring your emotions or pretending they don't exist—it's about finding a clear, purposeful path through the storm. Navigating means taking action, but it is action grounded in mindfulness and awareness.

To navigate effectively, you need to ask yourself,

What do I need right now to move through this with grace?

This could mean reaching out for support, practicing self-care, or even setting boundaries. Navigating is about taking the next step, even when it feels hard. It's about choosing a direction that supports your emotional well-being, whether that's finding healthy ways to express your feelings or allowing yourself the time and space to heal. Navigating through an emotional storm doesn't mean rushing toward an end. It means moving forward one mindful step at a time.

Finally, the last compass point is **Balance**. Emotional storms can throw us off-center, but finding balance helps us regain equilibrium. Balance is about learning how to integrate our emotions without letting them overwhelm us. It's about finding harmony between acknowledging our feelings and taking care of our well-being.

Balance is a continual practice. It doesn't mean achieving perfection or never experiencing emotional turbulence again; rather, it's about cultivating a sense of steadiness even in the midst of chaos. You'll find balance by regularly checking in with yourself, engaging in self-care, and embracing the flexibility that comes with emotional growth. When you practice balance, you're better able to stay grounded and aligned, even when life throws another storm your way.

The four compass points—Reflect, Pause, Navigate, and Balance—create a guide to help you handle emotional challenges with strength and resilience. They teach you to respond thoughtfully, grow through difficulties, and find peace during tough times.

Real change happens when we take the tools we've learned and apply them to our lives. The RPNB method has helped people overcome emotional storms, break unhealthy cycles, and create meaningful change. Below are six stories of individuals who used different aspects of this approach to find resilience, clarity, and healing.

1. Sarah's Battle with Anxiety.

Sarah had always struggled with overwhelming anxiety, especially in high-pressure situations. She would spiral into worst-case scenarios. This would lead to sleepless nights and panic attacks. One day, in the middle of a stressful work meeting, she decided to **Pause**. She took a deep breath and silently counted to five before responding. This helped her regain control. Over time, she practiced mindful pauses before reacting to stressful situations. It ultimately allowed her to make calmer, more thoughtful decisions. Combined with a focus on **Balance**, meditation, and self-care,

Sarah transformed her relationship with anxiety. She learned to manage it instead of letting it control her.

2. David's Path to Overcoming Burnout.

David was a high-achieving lawyer who was very fond of working long hours, but it came at a cost. David's long working hours led to chronic exhaustion and a strained marriage. When he finally hit a breaking point, he took time to **Reflect** on why he was pushing himself so hard. He realized that deep down, he feared that slowing down meant failure. This reflection helped him redefine success, and he began incorporating **Balance** into his life. He started setting boundaries, scheduling downtime, and prioritizing relationships. Within months, he not only felt more energized but also rediscovered that both his career and personal life had started to get better.

3. Maria's Journey Through Grief.

When Maria lost her mother unexpectedly, she was consumed by grief and tried to keep busy to avoid feeling the pain. But one day, she forced herself to **Pause**. She sat with her emotions instead of running from them. That pause led to **Reflection**. She realized that suppressing her grief was only prolonging the healing process. She began journaling about her feelings, talking to a therapist, and allowing herself to grieve fully. The process was painful, but in embracing it, she found a sense of peace and was able to honor her mother's memory without being consumed by sorrow.

4. Alex's Recovery from a Toxic Relationship.

Alex had spent years in an emotionally abusive relationship, unsure of how to break free. The turning point came when he learned to **Navigate**. He made a plan, sought support from friends, and worked with a counselor to build the courage to leave. Once out, he struggled with self-doubt. However, when he started focusing on **Balance**, he started rebuilding his self-worth through self-care, new hobbies, and positive relationships. This helped him heal. Looking back, he saw that navigating the hardest decision of his life was what ultimately set him free.

5. Jessica's Struggle with Self-Doubt (Reflect & Navigate)

Jessica was her own worst critic. Every time she had an opportunity for growth, she told herself she wasn't good enough, regardless if it was a promotion or a new project. One day, she decided to **Reflect** on where these thoughts were coming from. She traced them back to childhood experiences where she was constantly told to "play it safe." Recognizing this pattern, she decided to **Navigate** differently. Instead of letting fear dictate her choices, she actively challenged her inner critic and started saying "yes" to opportunities. Over time, her confidence grew, and she stepped into leadership roles she once thought were impossible.

6. Mark's Anger Management Breakthrough (Pause & Reflect)

Mark had a short temper that often got him into trouble at work and in relationships. After a particularly heated argument with his wife, he knew something had to change. He started practicing **Pause**. Before reacting in anger, he would take three deep breaths. This small change allowed him to avoid impulsive outbursts. He also began to **Reflect** on his triggers, realizing that his anger was often rooted in feeling unheard. These insights helped him communicate better, improving both his marriage and his relationships at work.

These six individuals once struggled with anxiety, burnout, grief, toxic relationships, self-doubt, and anger. But by using the RPNB method they found a way forward. Whether it was Pausing for control, Reflecting for insight, Navigating better choices, and Balancing emotions. Their stories show that resilience isn't about avoiding hardships but facing them with awareness and strength. Transformation is possible when we take intentional steps toward healing, no matter how overwhelming life feels.

In the next chapter, we will take a deeper dive into the first and perhaps most crucial aspect of the RPNB method—**Pause**. As we've seen in these stories, taking a moment to stop and create space before reacting can be a powerful tool for regaining control over our emotions.

But what does it truly mean to pause? How can we cultivate this practice in our daily lives, especially when emotions feel overwhelming?

In the next section, we'll explore the science behind Reflection, practical techniques to learn deeper self-awareness, and real-life examples of how this powerful practice can help us recognize hidden patterns, process emotions, and make more intentional choices. By learning to reflect effectively, we can gain clarity, break free from reactive cycles, and navigate emotional storms with greater understanding and purpose.

Activity

The 6-5-4-3-2-1 Grounding Game

When anxiety takes over, it can feel like your thoughts are spiraling out of control. This quick and fun grounding exercise can help bring you back to the present moment by engaging your senses.

How to Play:

6 – Look around and name **six things** you can see.

5 – Touch **five things** around you.

4 – Listen for **four sounds** you can hear.

3 – Identify **three smells** you notice.

2 – Name **two things** you will get rid of.

1 – Acknowledge **one thing** you can taste. (A mint, gum, or just the taste in your mouth.)

This short activity shifts your focus away from anxious thoughts and grounds you in the present. Try it next time anxiety strikes. You might be surprised how quickly it helps.

Chapter 2:
Reflect – Understanding the Root of Emotions

Have you ever found yourself reacting strongly to a situation and later wondering why it affected you so deeply?

That's what happens when we are triggered emotionally. Emotional triggers are like invisible tripwires. Certain words, situations, or interactions set off intense emotional responses before we even realize what's happening. Understanding these triggers and recognizing emotional patterns is key to gaining control over our reactions and breaking free from unhelpful cycles. The best way to understand your mind is through Reflection.

Reflecting is a detailed process with many stages and steps. In this chapter, I have collected six ways to help you understand it more. This is not a standard method to do it but it helps me. This is also not a step-by-step process. You can start from anywhere you feel comes naturally to you. Remember, this is not a self-help book but a guide to help you learn what's best for you and how. You can shape it however you feel suits you best.

The first thing to do is **pay attention to strong emotional reactions**. This is one of the easiest ways to identify your emotional triggers is by noticing moments when you feel a sudden shift in emotion.

Do you feel anger rise when someone interrupts you?

Does anxiety creep in when you get constructive criticism?

These reactions are often signals pointing to deeper, unresolved feelings. If you ask these questions after or during the event (A moment when you have experienced strong emotions suddenly), then you will start to get a bit clear on what your emotional triggers are.

The second thing is to **trace back to the root cause**. Once you identify a trigger, ask yourself:

Where is this coming from?

Often, our triggers are tied to past experiences. For example, if being ignored makes you feel deeply upset, it could stem from childhood moments where you felt unseen or unheard. Recognizing the root cause helps you separate the past from the present.

The third this is to **look for repeating patterns**. Patterns often reveal themselves when we step back and look at the bigger picture. For example, if you frequently feel defensive in conversations, it may indicate a deeper fear of being judged or misunderstood.

Do you find yourself having the same emotional reaction in different situations?

Keeping a journal can help track these patterns over time, which in turn will help you reflect on them.

The fourth thing is to **notice physical cues**. Our bodies often react before our minds process emotions. A racing heart, clenched jaw, or tight shoulders can all signal emotional distress. The next time you feel physically tense, pause and ask yourself what emotion you're experiencing and what might have triggered it.

The fifth thing is to **ask yourself key questions**.

When you feel triggered, take a moment to reflect by asking:

What just happened that caused this reaction?

What emotions am I feeling right now?

Have I felt this way before in similar situations?

What belief or fear might be fueling this reaction?

When you ask yourself these questions, you reflect. Once you reflect, you understand how your mind and body connect and react together.

The sixth thing is to **shift from reaction to awareness**. The goal of identifying emotional triggers isn't to eliminate them overnight but to increase awareness. Once you recognize your triggers and patterns, you gain the power to pause, reflect, and choose a different response. Even if you still do act impulsively, it's okay. Once the situation has passed, you can think about it with this different perspective. Once you're practicing reflection, you can step back and decide how you want to handle the situation while you're in it.

By uncovering your emotional triggers and patterns, you take an important step toward emotional resilience. Awareness is the first step to change, and with time, reflection, and practice, you can learn to navigate your emotions with greater clarity and control.

Sometimes, our emotions feel tangled, like a knot that's too tight. We sense frustration, sadness, or anxiety, but we can't quite pinpoint why. That's where guided journaling comes in. It is a simple yet powerful way to slow down, **reflect**, and uncover the deeper feelings beneath our reactions. Writing forces us to put thoughts into words, and in doing so, we often discover things we hadn't realized before.

Imagine sitting down with a blank page after a difficult conversation. You feel unsettled, but instead of pushing the feeling aside, you start writing.

What exactly happened?

What did I feel in that moment?

As you continue, the words start to flow. You realize it wasn't just about the conversation itself. It was about feeling unheard, something you've struggled with for years. By the time you finish, you don't just understand your emotions better. You feel lighter and more in control.

One thing that helps in reflection is journaling. Journaling is where you write whatever happened in your day. Major and minor. When I journaled for the first time, I couldn't think of anything. Even though I knew what to write, I didn't know how to write it. I'm sure many people go through the same thing. If you are one of those people, then worry not. This book is here to serve its purpose.

These are some prompts you can use to start your journaling journey:

What emotions have been coming up for me lately?

(List them without judgment.)

What situations tend to trigger these emotions?

(Be as specific as possible.)

When was the first time I remember feeling this way?

(Look for connections to past experiences.)

What is my inner dialogue when these emotions arise?

(Are you being self-critical, defensive, or compassionate?)

If my emotions could speak, what would they say?

(Let them express their needs.)

What do I need right now to feel more at peace?

(Actionable steps, big or small.)

Know that there are no right or wrong answers. Only honesty. The goal is to observe and **reflect** on your thoughts, not judge them. Over time, journaling helps create clarity. It reveals patterns and hidden emotions that shape the way we react to the world. The more we write, the more we understand ourselves. And with understanding comes healing.

Another thing to practice while reflecting is **Affirmations for Building Self-Awareness**.

Our thoughts shape the way we see ourselves and the world around us. When we're stuck in cycles of self-doubt, negativity, or fear, it's often because of the unconscious beliefs we've carried for years. Affirmations help shift those beliefs, replacing automatic, self-critical thoughts with intentional, empowering ones. By repeating affirmations regularly, we train our minds to focus on truth, growth, and self-awareness.

At first, affirmations might feel strange. Almost like saying words that don't quite belong to you yet. But over time, they start to take root. Instead of thinking,

I always mess up,

you remind yourself,

I am learning and growing every day.

Instead of

I'm not good enough,

you affirm,

I am worthy just as I am.

These small shifts in language have a powerful impact on self-awareness. They help us notice the negative stories we tell ourselves and rewrite them into something healthier.

This, paired with journaling, can also help you observe your self-talk (how you talk to yourself).

Here are some general examples of affirmations one can use:

I honor my emotions and allow myself to feel without judgment.

I am open to understanding myself on a deeper level.

Every experience is an opportunity for self-growth and learning.

I trust myself to navigate my emotions with wisdom and patience.

I release the need for perfection and embrace who I am in this moment.

My thoughts do not define me; I have the power to choose new ones.

Saying these affirmations out loud in the morning, writing them in a journal, or even keeping them as reminders on your phone can help reinforce them. The more we practice, the more we reshape our inner dialogue, fostering a deeper connection with ourselves and a greater sense of self-awareness.

Next are six stories of transformation through Reflection, Affirmations, and Journaling.

1. Maya – Learning to Accept Myself

For as long as I can remember, I felt like I wasn't enough. No matter how much I accomplished, self-doubt followed me everywhere. One day, I decided to journal every negative thought I had about myself. Seeing them on paper was a shock. I would never speak to a friend the way I spoke to myself. That's when I started using the affirmation: *I am enough just as I am.* At first, it felt forced, but over time, I started believing it. Now, when self-doubt creeps in, I remind myself of my worth.

2. Daniel – Breaking Free from Anger

I used to have a short fuse, snapping at people over the smallest things. One day, after yet another argument with my brother, I sat down to journal what had really set me off. As I wrote, it hit me. My anger wasn't just about him. It was about years of feeling ignored. I realized I had been carrying old wounds into new situations. That awareness changed everything. Now, before reacting, I take a deep breath and repeat: *I am heard, I am valued.* It helps me respond with clarity instead of emotion.

3. Priya – Overcoming Imposter Syndrome

Even after landing my dream job, I felt like a fraud. Every achievement felt like luck, not skill. One night, I started journaling about my successes, listing everything I had worked for. I noticed a pattern. I had been dismissing my own hard work. I started using the affirmation: *I am capable and deserving of success.* Each morning, I repeated it in the mirror. Over time, I began owning my accomplishments instead of shrinking from them.

4. Eric – Letting Go of the Fear of Failure

I always played it safe. The idea of failing terrified me, so I avoided anything that felt like a risk. But when I started journaling about my fears, I realized something: I had been told as a kid that mistakes meant I wasn't trying hard enough. That belief was still controlling me. I decided to challenge it with the affirmation that *I am allowed to grow and learn through failure.* It helped me take small risks, and eventually, bigger ones. Now, failure doesn't scare me—it fuels me.

5. Sofia – Healing from a Toxic Relationship

After leaving a toxic relationship, I felt broken. I journaled about my emotions every night, and one question kept coming up: *Why did I stay so long?* Writing helped me see how deeply I had believed that I wasn't worthy of real love. That's when I started using the affirmation: *I deserve love, respect, and kindness.* At first, it felt foreign. But with time, I started believing it. Now, I choose relationships that nurture me instead of draining me.

6. Jonah – Learning Self-Compassion

I used to be my own worst critic. If I made a mistake, I'd beat myself up for days. Then, one evening, I tried something different—I wrote myself a letter as if I were comforting a friend. It felt strange at first, but when I reread it, I realized I needed to show myself the same kindness I gave others. Now, I repeat: *I treat myself with the same kindness I give to others.* And for the first time, I feel lighter.

Each of them went on a journey of **reflection, affirmations, and journaling**, uncovering beliefs we didn't even realize were holding us back. These practices helped us see ourselves more clearly, challenge old narratives, and rewrite the stories we tell ourselves.

Activity:

The butterfly Hug.

The butterfly hug is a way to help you deal with overwhelming emotions.

It starts with you lying down in a comfortable place and then wrapping your arms around you in a way that you hug yourself. When you do it, your elbows and arms form a shape similar to a butterfly's wings, hence the name.

Slowly soothe yourself with your hands and let out a slow exhale. This will help you calm down physically. Try it whenever you feel intense frustration or other overwhelming emotions.

Chapter 3:
Pause – Creating Space for Stillness

Emotions can be powerful. They can shape our perceptions, influence our decisions, and even dictate our reactions. While emotions are natural and essential to human experience, they can also become overwhelming. This leads to impulsive actions or clouded judgment.

Pausing when emotions become too intense is a crucial skill that allows people to regain control. It helps them process their feelings and respond in a way that aligns with their values rather than their immediate impulses. In moments of heightened emotion, whether it be anger, sadness, or fear, taking a step back can prevent regret and foster emotional resilience.

One of the primary benefits of pausing is the ability to gain perspective. When emotions run high, they can distort reality, which, ultimately, makes situations seem more severe or personal than they actually are. By pausing, we create a mental space to assess the situation objectively.

This moment of Pause helps differentiate between what is a genuine issue and what might be an exaggerated reaction fueled by stress, past experiences, or external pressures. When we pause, we allow our rational mind to catch up with our emotional state, leading to clearer thinking and better decision-making.

Pausing also plays a vital role in effective communication. In moments of emotional overwhelm, we tend to say things without thinking or do things without a second thought. This is particularly true in conflicts, where an immediate emotional response can escalate tensions rather than resolve them.

By pausing, people process their emotions privately, reducing the likelihood of saying something hurtful or making a decision they might later regret. This simple act enables to create healthier relationships, as it encourages patience, understanding, and thoughtful dialogue.

From a psychological standpoint, pausing when you're overwhelmed can help regulate the nervous system. Emotional surges, especially those tied to stress or anxiety, activate the body's fight-or-flight response, leading to increased heart rate, shallow breathing, and heightened tension.

Pausing allows time for deep breathing and grounding techniques that help calm the nervous system, making it easier to respond rather than react. Over time, practicing this pause strengthens emotional self-regulation, making it easier to manage stress and maintain emotional stability.

Moreover, taking a pause builds self-awareness and emotional intelligence. By acknowledging intense emotions rather than immediately acting on them, individuals can better understand their triggers and patterns. This self-awareness leads to personal growth, as it enables individuals to identify recurring emotional themes and address underlying issues rather than merely reacting to surface-level triggers.

This practice can be especially beneficial in high-stakes environments such as the workplace, relationships, or decision-making scenarios where emotional intelligence is crucial.

Incorporating intentional pauses into daily life is a valuable skill that enhances both personal and professional well-being. Whether through mindful breathing, stepping away from a situation, or simply taking a moment to collect one's thoughts, pausing allows for a more measured and intentional response.

By creating this habit, people can deal with emotional challenges with greater clarity, ultimately leading to more constructive interactions and a healthier emotional state. In a fast-paced world that often demands instant reactions, the ability to pause is a quiet yet powerful form of self-mastery.

When emotions become overwhelming, grounding techniques can help bring awareness back to the present moment and restore a sense of stability.

Grounding is particularly useful during moments of high stress, anxiety, or emotional intensity, as it allows you to calm your nervous system and regain control of your thoughts and actions.

There are many effective grounding techniques, including breathing exercises, mindfulness, sensory focus, movement, and cognitive strategies. Each method offers a different approach to reconnecting with the present, making it easier to find relief from distressing emotions.

1. Breathing Exercises

Breathing exercises are one of the most accessible and effective ways to ground yourself. By focusing on slow, intentional breaths, the body's stress response can be regulated, reducing feelings of panic or emotional overwhelm.

Box Breathing (4-4-4-4 Method): Inhale for four seconds, hold for four seconds, exhale for four seconds, and hold again for four seconds. This method helps slow down rapid breathing and promotes a sense of calm.

4-7-8 Breathing: Inhale for four seconds, hold for seven seconds, and exhale for eight seconds. This technique slows the heart rate and encourages relaxation.

Diaphragmatic Breathing (Belly Breathing): Place one hand on the chest and one on the belly. Inhale deeply through the nose, expanding the belly, then exhale slowly through the mouth. This type of breathing stimulates the parasympathetic nervous system, which counters the stress response.

Alternate Nostril Breathing: Close one nostril, inhale through the other, then switch. This technique balances the nervous system and enhances focus.

Focusing on the breath not only slows down the physiological effects of stress but also redirects attention away from distressing thoughts, making it an essential grounding tool.

2. Mindfulness Techniques

Mindfulness is the practice of being fully present and aware of your thoughts, emotions, and surroundings without judgment. By engaging in mindfulness techniques, you can detach from overwhelming emotions and observe your experience with a sense of calm detachment.

Body Scan Meditation: This involves mentally scanning the body from head to toe, noticing any tension or sensations without judgment. It helps bring awareness to the physical body and reduces emotional reactivity.

Observing Thoughts: Instead of trying to suppress overwhelming thoughts, mindfulness encourages observing them as if they were clouds passing by in the sky. This practice reduces their intensity and helps cultivate emotional balance.

Five Senses Check-In: Identify five things you can see, four you can touch, three you can hear, two you can smell, and one you can taste. This anchors attention to the present moment and diverts it from distressing emotions.

Mindful Walking: Paying attention to the sensation of each step, the rhythm of movement, and the feeling of the ground beneath the feet can create a sense of stability and calm.

Practicing mindfulness helps you develop a healthier relationship with your emotions by building acceptance and reducing impulsive reactions.

3. Sensory Focus Techniques

Using sensory experiences to ground oneself is highly effective in moments of anxiety or emotional distress. By engaging with the five senses, you can redirect focus from distressing thoughts to physical sensations.

Holding an Object: Gripping a textured object, such as a smooth stone, fabric, or stress ball, can provide a tangible point of focus.

Cold Water Therapy: Splashing cold water on the face, holding an ice cube, or taking a cold shower activates the body's calming response and can quickly reduce emotional intensity.

Aromatherapy: Smelling essential oils, such as lavender or peppermint, can provide a soothing effect and bring attention to the present.

Listening to Music: Engaging in music with a calming or rhythmic beat helps regulate emotions and shift focus away from distress.

Chewing Gum or Eating Mindfully: Paying attention to the texture and flavor of food can create a sense of grounding and presence.

Sensory grounding techniques are especially useful for individuals who feel detached or overwhelmed, as they provide an immediate and tangible way to reconnect with reality.

4. Movement-Based Grounding

Physical movement can be an effective way to channel excess emotional energy and create a sense of stability. Engaging in intentional movement helps regulate emotions and reconnect the mind and body.

Stretching or Yoga: Gentle movements, such as stretching or practicing yoga, release physical tension and promote relaxation.

Progressive Muscle Relaxation (PMR): This involves tensing and then releasing different muscle groups, helping to reduce physical and emotional tension.

Walking or Running: Physical activity helps process emotions, release built-up energy, and create a sense of grounding.

Dancing or Shaking: Engaging in free movement can help release tension and improve mood.

Movement-based techniques are particularly helpful for individuals who struggle with restlessness or heightened emotional energy.

5. Cognitive and Verbal Grounding Techniques

Sometimes, shifting mental focus through structured thoughts or verbal engagement can be an effective way to ground yourself.

Self-Talk and Affirmations: Repeating calming affirmations such as "I am safe," "This feeling will pass," or "I am in control" can provide reassurance and stability.

Counting or Reciting: Counting backward from 100, reciting song lyrics, or listing favorite things can engage the logical part of the brain, shifting attention away from distress.

Describing the Environment: Verbally naming objects in the room, colors, or specific details of surroundings can reinforce a sense of reality.

Using a Grounding Phrase: Creating a personal grounding phrase, such as "I am here, I am safe, I am present," can serve as an emotional anchor.

Cognitive techniques work well for individuals who respond to structured thinking and verbal engagement as a way to regain emotional balance.

6. Visualization Techniques

Visualization involves using mental imagery to create a sense of calm and security. This technique is especially useful for those who find comfort in imagination and guided mental exercises.

Safe Place Visualization: Close your eyes and picture a place where you feel completely safe and at peace. It could be a beach, a forest, or a childhood home. Engage all senses by imagining the sights, sounds, smells, and textures.

Color Breathing: Imagine breathing in a calming color (such as blue for relaxation) and exhaling a stressful color (such as gray or black). This technique reinforces the idea of releasing tension with each breath.

Guided Imagery: Listening to guided meditations or recordings that describe peaceful scenes can help redirect focus away from distress.

Visualization techniques work well for people who respond to mental imagery and creative thinking as a way to manage emotions and regain control.

Grounding techniques provide effective strategies for managing overwhelming emotions, reducing stress, and restoring a sense of control. Whether through breathing exercises, mindfulness, sensory focus, movement, or cognitive engagement, each method offers a unique approach to emotional regulation.

Regular practice of these techniques strengthens emotional resilience, making it easier to navigate difficult moments with clarity and stability. By incorporating grounding into daily routines, you can develop healthier coping mechanisms.

As usual, here are six stories that showcase the actual power of pausing:

1. The Executive Who Avoided a Costly Outburst

Lisa, a high-level executive at a marketing firm, was in a tense boardroom meeting when a colleague unfairly criticized her work. She felt the heat of anger rising and was seconds away from snapping back. But she paused and left the room.

That short break allowed her to respond professionally instead of defensively. Later, she realized that her initial impulse would have damaged her reputation and relationships at work. Pausing gave her the clarity to address the issue with a level head, which ultimately earned her respect.

2. The Mother Who Chose Patience Over Frustration

Emma, a single mother of two, was exhausted after a long day when her children started arguing over a toy. Her instinct was to raise her voice and put an end to the chaos. But instead, she paused, closed her eyes, and took a few deep breaths.

In that moment, she reminded herself that her kids just wanted her attention, not intentionally being difficult. That pause helped her shift from frustration to patience. Instead of yelling, she calmly separated them, helped them share, and avoided turning the evening into an unnecessary battle.

3. The Student Who Prevented an Anxiety Spiral

David is a university student preparing for his final exams. As he looked at his study notes, an overwhelming wave of anxiety hit him. The thoughts poured in. "What if he failed? What if I'm not smart enough?" His chest tightened, and his thoughts raced.

Before panic took over, he paused. He set down his notes, took slow, deep breaths, and told himself, "One step at a time." That short break helped him shift from a spiral of self-doubt to a more focused and practical mindset. Instead of shutting down, he organized his study plan and tackled one topic at a time.

4. The Nurse Who Maintained Compassion in Chaos

Maria is an emergency room nurse. One day, in the middle of a high-stress shift when, a patient's family member lashed out at her in frustration. Maria felt very irritated. She was doing her best under intense pressure.

But instead of reacting defensively, she paused. She inhaled deeply, reminded herself that the person was scared, not angry at *her*, and responded with kindness. That moment of pause transformed the situation; the family member softened, apologized, and worked with her instead of against her. Pausing helped Maria maintain both her professionalism and her empathy.

5. The Retiree Who Prevented a Family Rift

James is a retired veteran and has always been opinionated. During a family dinner, his nephew made a comment about politics that irritated him. James felt the urge to correct him, to argue.

But then he paused. He reminded himself that a single dinner wasn't the time to have a heated debate. He took a sip of his drink, shifted the conversation, and let it go. Later, he realized that pausing helped him preserve his relationship rather than letting an argument drive a wedge between them.

6. The Artist Who Overcame Creative Block

Sofia, a painter, had been struggling with a creative block for weeks. Every time she picked up a brush, frustration consumed her. She was on the verge of quitting for the day when she decided to pause.

Instead of forcing inspiration, she stepped away, went for a walk, and breathed in the fresh air. When she returned to her studio an hour later, she felt lighter. She started painting without overthinking, and suddenly, her creativity flowed again. That simple act of stepping away helped her break through the mental barrier.

Activity:

Balloon Pop Anger Release

This is a fun and physical way to let go of anger without hurting anyone or holding it in.

What You'll Need:

- A few balloons
- A marker
- A safe space to pop balloons (outside or on a soft surface)

How to Do It:

1. **Blow up a balloon** – Imagine it filling with all your anger, frustration, and stress.
2. **Write it out** – Using a marker, jot down words or doodles that represent what's making you angry. It could be a situation, a person (without naming names if you share space with others), or just scribbles that express your emotions.
3. **Linger** – Let the balloon linger around for a while. Try to identify what emotions you feel towards the balloon now.
4. **Take a deep breath** – Before you pop it, take a slow inhale and exhale.
5. **POP!** – Stomp on it, squeeze it, or use a pin to pop the balloon. Imagine your anger bursting away with it.
6. **Final Shake-Off** – Jump, shake your arms or stretch to release any lingering frustration physically.

This activity is playful, cathartic, and a good way to turn anger into a moment of release.

Chapter 4:
Navigate – Charting a Way Forward

Life presents us with constant challenges—unexpected news, difficult conversations, and moments of high pressure. How we handle these situations often determines our emotional well-being, relationships, and decision-making abilities. The difference between *reacting* and *responding* is subtle but crucial.

A reaction is immediate and often driven by emotions like fear, anger, or frustration. It bypasses thoughtful consideration and relies on instinct rather than reflection. On the other hand, a response is deliberate. It involves pausing, assessing the situation, and choosing a course of action aligned with our values and long-term goals.

The key to shifting from reacting to responding lies in building awareness, emotional regulation, and intentional decision-making.

Between what happens to us and how we choose to act, there exists a moment of choice. This space may seem temporary, but it is where our true power lies. By becoming aware of this gap, we can slow down our automatic reactions and make intentional choices.

When faced with a triggering situation, take a deep breath. A few seconds of mindfulness can create the space needed to shift from an impulsive reaction to a thoughtful response.

Pay attention to physical sensations and emotional signals. These can be a tightening feeling in the chest, clenching your fists, or a sudden surge of anger. These are signs that a reaction is forming.

Before speaking or acting, pause and ask: *What am I feeling? Why am I feeling this way? What outcome do I want?* This self-inquiry helps transition from automatic reaction to conscious response.

Emotions are not the enemy—uncontrolled emotions are. Regulating our emotions allows us to respond with clarity and composure rather than being hijacked by impulses.

Deep, slow breaths activate the parasympathetic nervous system, calming the body and allowing for clearer thinking. Research shows that simply labeling emotions (*I feel frustrated, I feel disappointed*) reduces their intensity and creates psychological distance.

Instead of seeing an event as a personal attack or crisis, reframe it as an opportunity to learn or a challenge to navigate with wisdom.

Once we've paused and regulated our emotions, the next step is choosing a response that aligns with our long-term values and goals.

Ask yourself, *Will this matter a year from now?* Shifting perspective helps avoid reactive decisions based on fleeting emotions.

Whether in conversations or conflicts, communicate with intention. Instead of lashing out, express your thoughts in a way that fosters understanding rather than conflict.

Have a plan for handling high-stress situations—whether it's stepping away for a moment, writing down your thoughts before speaking, or practicing a grounding exercise.

Making decisions that align with your values is essential for living a life of integrity, fulfillment, and purpose. However, in moments of uncertainty or pressure, it's easy to make choices that contradict our core beliefs. Whether influenced by emotions, societal expectations, or immediate gratification, misaligned decisions can lead to regret and internal conflict. To navigate life with clarity and confidence, it's crucial to develop strategies that ensure our choices reflect our deepest values.

The first step in value-based decision-making is identifying what truly matters to you. Your values serve as your internal compass, guiding your actions and helping you stay on course. Take time to define your top values—whether honesty, compassion, growth, or balance. Writing them down can provide clarity and serve as a reference when faced with difficult choices. It's also important to ensure these values are genuinely yours, not just inherited from family, culture, or societal expectations. A decision aligned with authentic values will always feel more fulfilling in the long run.

Once you have clarity on your values, applying the "10-10-10" rule can help assess decisions with a long-term perspective. This method involves asking yourself three questions: *How will I feel about this decision in 10 minutes? In 10 months? In 10 years?* While a choice may seem appealing in the moment, considering its future impact can help you avoid short-sighted decisions driven by temporary emotions. This strategy encourages patience and mindfulness, ensuring that your actions align with your long-term vision.

Another powerful technique is creating a decision-making pause. In high-pressure situations, people often react impulsively rather than responding thoughtfully. Instead of rushing into a choice, take a moment to breathe and assess the situation rationally. If possible, step away and give yourself time to think—whether that means sleeping on a decision, taking a walk, or discussing it with a trusted friend. Giving yourself space can prevent emotionally driven choices and allow you to make more deliberate, value-based decisions.

It's also essential to consider the ripple effect of your choices. Every decision influences not only your own life but also those around you. Before making a choice, ask yourself: *Who will this affect? Will this decision align with my future self? Will I be proud of this choice later?* Evaluating the broader consequences of your actions ensures that you are making responsible and thoughtful decisions that contribute positively to your life and relationships.

Finally, staying aligned with your values requires consistent follow-through. Once a decision is made, commit to it fully and take responsibility for your actions. If circumstances change and a past decision no longer aligns with your evolving values, allow yourself to adjust and make course corrections when necessary. Regular self-reflection—such as journaling or checking in with yourself—can help ensure that you remain true to your values over time.

By practicing these decision-making strategies, you can navigate life with greater confidence and purpose. Instead of being swayed by external pressures or fleeting emotions, you will make choices that honor your authentic self, leading to a more fulfilling and intentional life.

Navigating emotions effectively is a skill that requires practice, patience, and self-awareness. In high-stress or emotionally charged moments, the ability to pause, reflect, and respond with clarity can transform how we handle challenges. The following exercises are designed to strengthen your emotional resilience and improve your ability to respond intentionally rather than react impulsively.

1. Name and Reframe Your Emotions

Instead of being consumed by emotions, practice labeling them. Studies show that simply naming an emotion—such as frustration, disappointment, or anxiety—reduces its intensity.

- When you feel triggered, take a deep breath and say, *I am feeling __ right now.*
- Ask yourself: *Is there another way to interpret this situation?*
- Try reframing: Instead of *I am stuck*, say *I am in a transition period, and growth takes time.*

By naming and reframing emotions, you gain control over them instead of letting them control you.

2. The Pause-and-Respond Method

One of the simplest yet most powerful practices in emotional navigation is learning to pause before reacting. This technique helps you slow down impulsive responses and make decisions that align with your values.

- When faced with a difficult situation, take a **10-second pause** before responding.
- Use this moment to ask yourself: *What is the best response that aligns with my values?*
- If emotions are too strong, step away and revisit the conversation when you are calmer.

The more you practice pausing, the more natural it becomes to respond with clarity and intention.

3. Journaling for Emotional Clarity

Writing down your thoughts and emotions provides an outlet for self-reflection and problem-solving. This practice can help you process feelings and gain insight into recurring patterns in your reactions.

- Set aside **five minutes** each day to write about a challenging situation you experienced.
- Describe the emotions you felt and how you reacted.
- Ask yourself: *What could I have done differently?*

- Identify small adjustments you can make in future situations.

Over time, journaling helps build emotional intelligence and self-awareness, making it easier to navigate difficult emotions with confidence.

4. The "Third-Person Perspective" Exercise

Emotions often cloud our judgment, making it hard to see situations objectively. Viewing the problem from an outside perspective can help you detach from immediate emotional impulses.

- Imagine you are an observer watching your situation unfold.
- Ask yourself: *If I were giving advice to a friend in this situation, what would I say?*
- Consider how a neutral third party might view the scenario.

This technique allows you to step back from your emotions and approach challenges with greater wisdom and clarity.

5. The Breath-Anchor Technique

Your breath is a powerful tool for emotional regulation. In stressful moments, controlled breathing can activate the body's relaxation response and restore a sense of calm.

- Inhale deeply through your nose for **four seconds.**
- Hold your breath for **four seconds.**
- Exhale slowly through your mouth for **six seconds.**
- Repeat this cycle **four to five times.**

This simple exercise can be practiced anytime you feel overwhelmed, helping to reset your emotional state and approach the situation with a clear mind.

6. Visualizing Your Ideal Response

Before entering a challenging conversation or situation, take a few moments to rehearse your response mentally.

- Close your eyes and visualize yourself handling the situation with composure.

- Imagine speaking calmly, listening actively, and responding thoughtfully.
- Focus on how you want to feel after the situation—confident, in control, and aligned with your values.

This mental preparation primes your brain for a more measured response when the actual moment arrives.

By incorporating these exercises into your daily routine, you can strengthen your ability to navigate emotions with grace and intention. Emotional resilience is a skill that grows with practice, allowing you to face life's challenges with confidence and clarity.

As it has become a ritual, here are six personal stories that illustrate emotional navigation and decision-making aligned with values. Each story highlights a real-life challenge and how thoughtful responses, rather than impulsive reactions, led to meaningful outcomes.

1. The Silent Apology

Emma had a heated argument with her younger sister over something trivial. In the past, she would have snapped back instantly, but this time, she paused. Instead of reacting with anger, she took a deep breath, walked away, and reflected. The next morning, rather than forcing an apology, she made her sister breakfast and left a small note saying, *I love you.* Her sister responded with a hug. Sometimes, an intentional act speaks louder than words.

2. The Job Offer Dilemma

Jason was offered a higher-paying job that required frequent travel, but it clashed with his core value of family time. Tempted by the financial benefits, he almost said yes. However, he paused to reflect: *Will this decision align with my long-term happiness?* After considering the impact on his wife and kids, he turned down the offer. A few months later, a remote leadership role opened at his current company, allowing him to grow professionally while staying close to his family.

3. The Public Embarrassment

Sophia, a university student, was called out by her professor for an incomplete assignment in front of her peers. Her initial reaction was to lash out in frustration, but instead, she took a deep breath and responded, *You're right. I should have planned better. I'll submit it by tomorrow.* Later, her professor acknowledged her maturity and offered mentorship, a relationship that helped Sophia excel in her career.

4. The Unsent Message

Daniel's best friend ghosted him after years of friendship, leaving him feeling hurt and betrayed. One night, he drafted a long, angry message demanding an explanation. Just before hitting send, he asked himself, *What outcome do I truly want?* Realizing he didn't need closure from someone who didn't respect him, he deleted the message. Instead of reacting, he redirected his energy toward strengthening his relationships with people who valued him.

5. The Customer Service Challenge

Lena worked at a busy café and had a rude customer who insulted her over a wrong order. Her instinct was to defend herself, but instead, she smiled and said, *I see that you're upset. Let me fix this for you right away.* The customer softened instantly, apologized, and left a generous tip. Choosing to respond with kindness instead of reacting with frustration changed the entire dynamic.

6. The Unexpected Detour

Mark's flight was canceled last minute, ruining his vacation plans. His first reaction was to get angry, but instead, he took a deep breath and reframed his perspective: *What's the best alternative?* Instead of wasting energy on frustration, he booked a spontaneous road trip to a nearby city. That trip ended up being one of his most memorable experiences.

Activity

The "Release & Reset" Method

This activity helps you feel better when you're frustrated. The objective of this activity is to quickly process and release frustration in a healthy way, so you can respond thoughtfully instead of reacting impulsively.

Step 1: Identify the Frustration (1 Minute)

- Write down or say out loud: *What exactly is frustrating me?*
- Be specific: Is it a situation, a person, or an unmet expectation?

Step 2: Physical Release (2 Minutes)

- Choose a quick physical action to release tension:
  - Take five deep breaths, inhaling for 4 seconds and exhaling for 6.
  - Shake out your hands or do 10 jumping jacks.
  - Press your palms together and hold for 5 seconds, then release.

Step 3: Mental Reset (2 Minutes)

- Ask yourself: *Is this in my control?*
  - If yes, brainstorm one small step you can take.
  - If no, remind yourself: *I can't control this, but I can control my response.*
- Use a reframing statement:
  - Instead of *This is so unfair*, say *This is challenging, but I'll find a way through it.*

Step 4: Intentional Action (1 Minute)

- Decide how you will respond.
- If needed, take a break before engaging in the situation again.

This quick activity helps shift frustration from a reactive state to a place of clarity and control. Would you like variations for specific scenarios?

Chapter 5:
Balance – Restoring Harmony in Life

Maintaining balance in today's fast-paced world requires effort in doing self-care, making routines, and setting boundaries. Self-care lays the foundation by ensuring that physical, emotional, and mental needs are met, allowing individuals to function with clarity and resilience. Routines build on this by introducing structure and predictability into daily life, reducing stress and fostering healthy habits over time. Boundaries, meanwhile, act as safeguards that protect one's energy and priorities by setting clear limits in relationships, work, and personal commitments. Together, these three elements create a stable framework that supports well-being and helps individuals lead more intentional, balanced lives.

To truly understand what it means to live a balanced life, it's essential to look at the practices that support our overall well-being. While balance can look different for everyone, it consistently begins with how we care for ourselves on the most fundamental level. Before we can manage responsibilities or support others, we need to ensure our own physical, emotional, and mental health is tended to. This is where self-care plays a pivotal role, as the first and most personal step toward building a sustainable, fulfilling life.

Self-care refers to the intentional actions we take to preserve or improve our physical, emotional, and mental well-being. It's not just about pampering—it's a foundational practice that helps us manage stress, prevent burnout, and maintain resilience.

Physical self-care consists of sleep, nutrition, exercise, etc. It supports energy levels, immune function, and overall stamina. It ensures the body can meet daily demands. Emotional self-care involves journaling, therapy, and sometimes talking to a friend. This helps one process feelings, reduce emotional overwhelm, and stay connected to one's inner world. Finally, mental self-care keeps your mind stimulated and grounded, helping prevent anxiety and mental fatigue. Common methods include reading, learning, and practicing mindfulness.

Self-care replenishes your inner resources so that you do not operate from a place of depletion. It empowers you to respond to life's challenges rather than react impulsively.

Once a strong foundation of self-care is in place, the next step is creating consistency through routines. While self-care helps us recharge, routines provide the structure needed to keep that energy focused and steady throughout the day. They bring a sense of order and rhythm to our lives, making it easier to stay on track with goals, manage time effectively, and reduce the mental load of constant decision-making. In this way, routines become the practical tools that transform self-care into lasting, daily support.

A routine is a sequence of actions regularly followed. While it can sound rigid, a healthy routine creates rhythm and predictability, both of which are psychologically calming.

Having a regular schedule reduces decision fatigue and mental clutter, freeing up energy for more meaningful tasks. Routines reinforce healthy habits like regular sleep, focused work time, or exercise, which accumulate into long-term benefits. When life feels uncertain or stressful, routines offer a sense of control and grounding.

Routines act as mental scaffolding, giving your day direction and purpose. This reduces stress and helps you move through life with more intention and less overwhelm.

With both self-care and routines working together to support our well-being and productivity, the final key to maintaining true balance lies in setting healthy boundaries. Even the best self-care practices and structured routines can quickly unravel if we don't protect our time, energy, and values. Boundaries act as a protective barrier, helping us define what is acceptable and sustainable in our relationships, work commitments, and personal space. By setting clear limits, we make room for what truly matters— preserving the balance we've worked hard to build.

Boundaries are the limits you set to protect your time, energy, values, and emotional well-being. They can be physical, emotional, digital, or relational.

Saying no when needed protects your time and prevents over-commitment. Clear boundaries reduce resentment and confusion in relationships by clarifying expectations. Boundaries affirm your worth and help you prioritize your needs without guilt.

Boundaries create space for what truly matters. They help you avoid feeling stretched too thin and ensure you're investing your energy in ways that align with your values.

While self-care, routines, and boundaries lay the groundwork for a balanced life, maintaining that balance over time requires intentional periods of restoration. Even with healthy habits in place, the demands of daily life can slowly drain our emotional, mental, and physical energy. To truly sustain well-being, it's important to recognize when we need to pause and replenish. This is where restorative practices come in—offering targeted ways to recover, reset, and return to ourselves with renewed strength and clarity.

Restoration is essential for sustaining health and resilience, especially in a world that constantly demands our attention and energy. True restoration involves more than just sleep or occasional breaks—it requires intentional practices that target emotional, mental, and physical well-being. When these areas are nurtured in harmony, we feel more grounded, present, and capable of handling life's challenges.

Emotional Restoration often begins with creating space to feel and process emotions. Practices like journaling, speaking with a trusted friend or therapist, or engaging in creative expression—such as art, music, or dance—can help release suppressed feelings and provide clarity. Spending time in emotionally safe environments, setting aside moments for reflection, and practicing self-compassion are also powerful ways to replenish emotional reserves.

Mental Restoration focuses on quieting the mind and reducing cognitive overload. Meditation, deep breathing exercises, or simply unplugging from screens for a few hours can significantly reduce mental fatigue. Engaging in mentally stimulating yet calming activities—like reading fiction, walking in nature, or doing puzzles—helps the brain reset and shift out of problem-solving mode. Adequate sleep and mindful breaks during the day are also crucial for restoring mental sharpness and focus.

Physical Restoration centers on rest, movement, and nourishment. This might include getting sufficient high-quality sleep, taking naps when needed, or engaging in gentle physical activity like yoga, stretching, or walking. Hydrating, eating nutrient-dense meals, and allowing the body time to heal after illness or stress are all forms of physical care that restore strength and vitality. Listening to bodily cues—such as fatigue, tension, or pain—and responding with kindness is a vital part of long-term physical well-being.

Together, these restorative practices create a well-rounded system of care. When we prioritize restoration across emotional, mental, and physical dimensions, we build the inner reserves needed to live with energy, clarity, and emotional balance.

After making space for restoration, one powerful way to reinforce inner balance is through the practice of affirmations. Affirmations are intentional, positive statements that help shift our mindset, align our thoughts with our values, and cultivate emotional harmony. When used consistently, they can reduce negative self-talk, build confidence, and create a sense of inner peace, especially when we feel overwhelmed or disconnected. By speaking to ourselves with kindness and intention, we strengthen our relationship with our inner world.

Affirmations work by gently rewiring our thoughts, helping us replace patterns of doubt, fear, or stress with clarity, calm, and self-compassion. They serve as reminders of our worth, our ability to handle challenges, and our right to peace and balance. Whether spoken aloud, written down, or silently repeated, affirmations become grounding tools we can return to anytime we feel off-center.

Some of the affirmations written below can be helpful.

"I am grounded, calm, and centered no matter what is happening around me."

"I trust myself to make decisions that honor my well-being."

"It is safe for me to set boundaries and prioritize my needs."

"I release what I cannot control and focus on what I can."

"I am worthy of rest, joy, and kindness—just as I am."

"Each breath I take brings me closer to peace and clarity."

These affirmations help you remain steady and connected to yourself during stressful moments. They encourage self-trust and confidence in choosing what's best for your health and peace. They also validate the importance of boundaries in creating emotional balance. Affirmations aid in letting go of anxiety caused by external pressures or uncertainty. They reinforce self-worth without conditions or productivity.

Incorporating these affirmations into a daily routine, perhaps during morning reflection, meditation, or bedtime, can create a consistent inner dialogue rooted in calm and self-acceptance.

Affirmations can be a powerful tool for personal growth and emotional well-being because they directly influence how we speak to ourselves and how we see ourselves. Our inner dialogue has a profound impact on our confidence, choices, and even how we respond to stress or setbacks. When we use affirmations consistently, we begin to reshape that inner voice from one that may be critical or doubtful into one that is supportive, empowering, and compassionate.

One of the biggest ways affirmations help is by challenging negative self-talk. Many people carry subconscious beliefs like "I'm not good enough" or "I always mess things up." Affirmations such as "I am capable and learning every day" gently counter those thoughts and offer a new, more constructive narrative.

Affirmations also help by creating focus and intention. When you repeat an affirmation like "I am calm and in control," especially during moments of anxiety, you're not just reciting words—you're anchoring yourself in the mindset you want to adopt. Over time, this practice rewires your thinking patterns, reducing reactivity and promoting emotional balance.

Additionally, affirmations promote self-awareness and alignment with values. They remind you of what matters most, whether that's inner peace, confidence, gratitude, or resilience. Used daily, affirmations become more than positive statements. They become guideposts for how you live, react, and relate to yourself and others.

In short, affirmations are a simple but transformative practice that helps you shift your mindset, reduce negativity, and build a more compassionate and empowered relationship with yourself

Let's read six stories where balancing was the superhero in people's lives.

1. Anna's Morning Reset (Self-Care)

Anna, a graphic designer, found herself snapping at coworkers and skipping meals during tight deadlines. Realizing she was neglecting her own needs, she committed to 15 minutes of quiet time each morning with tea and a nourishing breakfast. This small self-care ritual gave her the grounding she needed to approach work with more patience and presence, dramatically improving her mood and focus.

2. Jamal's Study Rhythm (Routine)

Jamal, a university student, struggled with staying focused and often pulled all-nighters before exams. After a frustrating semester, he created a simple study routine: three 45-minute sessions each day, broken up by movement or snack breaks. The structure helped reduce his anxiety and kept his mind fresh, and for the first time, he finished a term without cramming or burning out.

3. Priya's Gentle No (Boundaries)

Priya was the go-to person in her friend group—always saying yes to late-night calls and last-minute favors. Eventually, she felt drained and resentful. With encouragement from a counselor, she practiced saying no kindly but firmly. Setting these boundaries didn't harm her relationships; in fact, it led to deeper respect and gave her back the space she needed to enjoy social time again.

4. Malik's Midday Walks (Restoration)

Working remotely had blurred all lines for Malik, who rarely took breaks and felt constantly fatigued. He started taking a 20-minute walk outside every afternoon with no phone or agenda. The fresh air and movement helped clear his mind, reduce screen fatigue, and restored his energy to tackle the second half of his day more productively.

5. Elina's Mirror Notes (Affirmations)

Elina struggled with self-doubt before presentations. She began writing affirmations on sticky notes and placing them on her mirror: "I speak with confidence and clarity." Repeating them aloud each morning gradually shifted her mindset. Over time, her nervousness lessened, and she began receiving positive feedback on her delivery and presence.

6. Theo's Sunday Evenings (All Three Combined)

Theo, a busy single dad, felt like the week always ran him instead of the other way around. He started dedicating Sunday evenings to planning the week, journaling, and doing something relaxing like watching a favorite show. This intentional time blended routine, self-care, and reflection, which made his weeks feel less chaotic and more manageable.

Each of these stories highlights how small, intentional practices can bring balance and resolve everyday stresses.

Activity

"The Sadness Letter"

Purpose:
To acknowledge and release sadness through expression, reflection, and self-compassion.

Instructions:

1. Find a quiet, comfortable space where you won't be interrupted for 10–15 minutes. Bring a journal or a piece of paper and a pen.

2. Take a few deep breaths to center yourself. Let your body relax and your mind settle.

3. Write a letter to your sadness as if it were a person. Begin with: *"Dear Sadness, I see you..."*

   Allow yourself to freely express:

   - What the sadness feels like
   - Where you think it's coming from
   - What you want it to know
   - What you need from yourself or others right now

4. Read the letter aloud to yourself slowly, with kindness. If emotions rise, let them. You're safe to feel.

5. Finish with a closing affirmation, such as:

   "I am allowed to feel. I am healing, and I am not alone."

Optional: You can keep the letter, tear it up, or burn it (safely) as a symbolic release, whatever feels most comforting.

Chapter 6:
Reframing Challenges – Turning Storms into Strength

Life is full of challenges, disappointments, and unexpected turns, but how we respond to these moments can define our path forward. While it's natural to feel discouraged in the face of failure or pain, there is immense power in learning to reframe negative experiences into meaningful lessons. This mindset shift doesn't deny the difficulty of a situation; instead, it transforms it into a stepping stone for growth. Reframing is not about forced positivity; it's about choosing perspective with intention and purpose.

Reframing negative experiences into lessons is a powerful psychological tool that helps individuals find meaning in adversity and grow from hardship. Rather than viewing setbacks as failures, reframing allows us to reinterpret them as opportunities for learning and self-improvement. For example, instead of saying "I was rejected from that job because I'm not good enough," a person might reframe it as, "That job wasn't the right fit, and now I have a clearer idea of what I want and need to improve." This mental shift not only protects self-esteem but also builds resilience, which is the ability to bounce back and try again with renewed insight.

The key to successful reframing lies in conscious reflection. It requires asking constructive questions, such as, "What did I learn from this?" How can this make me stronger or wiser? What would I do differently next time? This introspective approach transforms passive suffering into active growth. Over time, consistently practicing reframing helps cultivate a growth mindset—a belief that abilities and intelligence can be developed through effort and experience.

Furthermore, neuroscience supports the benefits of reframing. Studies have shown that the brain can rewire itself through repeated thought patterns. By intentionally choosing more empowering interpretations of events, we strengthen neural pathways associated with optimism, problem-solving, and emotional regulation. In this way, reframing isn't just a mental trick—it becomes a long-term investment in psychological well-being.

In summary, reframing negative experiences into lessons is more than just positive thinking; it's a proactive and strategic approach to personal development. It encourages emotional maturity, reduces the power of regret, and equips individuals to navigate future challenges with clarity and courage. Rather than being defined by what went wrong, we are shaped by how we choose to respond.

Gratitude exercises work by gently guiding the mind away from what is missing or painful and toward what is present and nourishing. In a world where it's easy to become consumed by comparison, pressure, or negativity—especially through social media or high-stress environments— practicing gratitude creates a pause. It's a moment of acknowledgment that not everything is broken, even when parts of life feel that way. This perspective doesn't require life to be perfect; it simply asks us to notice what's already good. Whether it's the warmth of a morning cup of coffee, the support of a friend, or a quiet moment of peace, these small recognitions build emotional resilience over time.

One powerful form of this practice is called "savoring," which involves fully immersing yourself in a positive experience and mentally extending its impact. For instance, rather than rushing through a pleasant walk, you might slow down, notice the sunlight on your skin, the rhythm of your breath, or the sound of birds. Consciously appreciating these details magnifies the joy they offer and reinforces the brain's ability to find beauty in the ordinary.

Gratitude exercises also help in reframing difficult memories. For example, someone might reflect on a painful breakup but express gratitude for the self-awareness, independence, or emotional boundaries they gained through that experience. This doesn't negate the pain but adds layers of meaning that soften its edge and bring purpose to the healing process.

Ultimately, gratitude is not about ignoring problems—it's about widening our perspective. It allows us to see life in its fullness: the pain and the progress, the loss and the learning, the fear and the fortitude. When practiced consistently, gratitude becomes not just an exercise, but a mindset that enriches every aspect of life.

A few years ago, a young woman named Lina faced one of the most challenging periods of her life. She had just moved to a new city to begin a promising job when, within months, everything seemed to unravel. Her father was diagnosed with a serious illness back home, her work performance suffered under the emotional strain, and the isolation of living in a new place with no close friends left her feeling helpless. It felt like life had cornered her—personally, professionally, and emotionally.

At first, Lina tried to push through by ignoring her feelings. However, the stress became too great to conceal. Eventually, she took a step back and gave herself permission to slow down. She reached out to a local support group and began practicing simple gratitude exercises every morning—listing three things, no matter how small, that were still okay. One day, it was just "a good cup of tea, a short walk, and my sister's text." Another day, it was "the fact that I got out of bed today." These small acknowledgments slowly grounded her.

As she cared for her emotional well-being, she began to reframe her situation. Rather than seeing it as a season of failure, she chose to view it as a time of rebuilding and learning endurance. She began journaling about the skills she was developing, including how to ask for help, sit with discomfort, and stay present in the face of uncertainty. Eventually, Lina found her footing. Her father's condition stabilized, she adjusted to her role at work, and she built meaningful connections in her new community.

Looking back, Lina doesn't pretend that time wasn't painful—but she sees it as one of her greatest teachers. Her resilience wasn't about being unshaken; it was about staying open, adaptable, and grounded through the storm. Her story shows that resilience isn't a trait only some people are born with—it's something we can all build, moment by moment, choice by choice.

Challenges are an inevitable part of life, but how we choose to interpret them can make all the difference. While it's easy to feel defeated in the face of setbacks, many people discover unexpected strength and opportunity when they shift their perspective. Reframing challenges isn't about denying pain or pretending everything is fine—it's about finding meaning, growth, or new direction within the struggle. The following six mini-stories highlight real examples of individuals who turned difficult moments into powerful turning points simply by changing how they viewed their circumstances.

1. The Missed Flight That Became a Pause

Jared missed his connecting flight due to a delay, leaving him stranded in a foreign airport overnight. At first, he was furious—he had a big presentation the next morning. But as he sat there, he realized how exhausted he'd been from nonstop travel. He used the unexpected time to rest, reset his slides, and even journal. When he finally arrived, he gave one of his best presentations, calmer and more focused than ever.

2. From Injury to New Passion

Maya, a lifelong runner, tore a ligament and was told she might never run competitively again. Devastated, she spiraled into sadness—until a friend invited her to a yoga class. What began as a reluctant experiment turned into a new passion. Within a year, she became a certified instructor, finding peace and purpose in a practice she'd never have explored otherwise.

3. Job Rejection, Career Redirection

Ali had dreamed of working for a prestigious tech company and made it to the final interview, only to be rejected. Crushed, he spent weeks doubting himself. However, during that time, he also began helping a friend build a small app, something he'd never considered before. That side project evolved into a startup, and three years later, he was hiring his own team, which included someone from the very same tech company.

4. A Failed Exam and a New Strategy

Sofia failed a critical licensing exam she had spent months preparing for. She initially saw it as a sign that she wasn't smart enough. But after speaking with others who had also failed and later passed, she reframed the experience as a learning opportunity. She changed her study approach, worked with a mentor, and passed on her second try, this time with a deeper understanding and stronger confidence.

5. Losing a Friend, Finding Self-Respect

Tom had a falling out with a longtime friend after setting a boundary about how he was being treated. He grieved the loss but realized the friendship had been draining him for years. Reframing the pain as an act of self-respect helped him heal and build healthier relationships moving forward.

6. Public Speaking Panic Turned Practice

When Anika froze during a school presentation, she was mortified. She considered avoiding public speaking forever. But her teacher encouraged her to view the moment not as a failure, but as a first step. Anika joined a speaking club, practiced weekly, and eventually won an award for best speaker in her final year. What once embarrassed her became a source of pride.

Activity

"Letters of Love" – A Gentle Grief Writing Practice

This reflective activity allows you to process grief by expressing unspoken thoughts, memories, or emotions through writing. It's a quiet, healing way to stay connected to a loved one or come to peace with a loss.

Instructions:

1. Find a quiet space where you feel safe and won't be interrupted. Have a notebook or piece of paper ready.

2. Write a letter to the person or thing you're grieving. You can begin with "Dear…" and let the words flow. You might want to share:

   a. A memory that brings you comfort.

   b. Something you didn't get to say.

   c. How their presence shaped you.

   d. How you're doing now, honestly.

3. No rules—just honesty. You don't need perfect grammar or structure. Let your emotions lead. If you're angry, be angry. If you're grateful, express your thanks.

4. Close the letter however feels right—whether with a goodbye, 'see you soon,' or simply your name.

5. **Optional step:** You may choose to keep, bury, burn, or place the letter somewhere meaningful. This symbolic act can provide a sense of closure or connection.

This exercise doesn't erase grief, but it gives your heart a voice and creates space for healing through remembrance, expression, and release.

Chapter 7:
Building Your Emotional Toolbox

In times of stress, uncertainty, or emotional overwhelm, having reliable tools to ground and restore yourself is essential. Emotional resilience isn't just about "being tough." It's about building the mental and emotional habits that help you recover, adapt, and stay steady through life's ups and downs. Fortunately, resilience can be cultivated through simple, consistent practices that train your mind to respond with calm, clarity, and self-compassion. Among the most effective tools are meditation, affirmations, visualization, and gratitude. Each offers a unique way to strengthen your inner world, helping you stay connected to your values, centered in your body, and anchored in hope—even when everything else feels uncertain. Let's explore how each of these practices can support you.

Meditation is one of the most effective tools for building emotional resilience because it trains the mind to observe thoughts without becoming overwhelmed by them. In moments of stress, our minds tend to spiral—jumping from fear to doubt to frustration. Meditation creates space between stimulus and response, helping us pause before reacting. Even just 5–10 minutes a day of quiet, focused breathing or guided mindfulness can reduce anxiety, lower cortisol levels, and improve emotional regulation.

Over time, meditation strengthens the brain's prefrontal cortex—the area responsible for decision-making and self-control—while calming the amygdala, which governs the fight-or-flight response. Whether through breath awareness, body scans, or loving-kindness practices, meditation helps us respond to challenges with clarity and calm, rather than panic or emotional reactivity. It doesn't remove hardship, but it equips us to face it with a steady, grounded mind.

While meditation helps quiet the mind and create space between thought and reaction, affirmations take that inner stillness a step further by intentionally shaping the thoughts that fill that space. Once we've learned to observe our thoughts through meditation, we become more aware of the patterns—especially the self-critical or fearful ones—that may be undermining our confidence. Affirmations offer a way to gently replace those patterns with empowering, supportive beliefs. They don't ignore reality—they strengthen our mindset so we can face it with greater self-trust.

Affirmations are positive, intentional statements that help reshape your internal dialogue. When practiced consistently, they challenge and replace negative self-talk, making space for a more empowering, supportive mindset. Emotional resilience often depends not just on what happens to us, but on what we tell ourselves about it. If your inner voice constantly says, "I can't handle this" or "I'm not enough," it chips away at confidence and stability. Affirmations work like mental anchors—reminders of your strength, worth, and capacity to cope.

Examples include:

"I am stronger than my circumstances."

"I trust myself to navigate this moment."

"It's okay to feel overwhelmed—I'm still moving forward."

Repeating affirmations aloud, writing them down, or posting them where you'll see them daily helps reinforce these beliefs. Over time, your subconscious begins to adopt these messages as truth, which can boost resilience in the face of stress, failure, or change. The goal isn't to fake confidence—it's to practice speaking to yourself with the same encouragement you'd offer a friend.

As affirmations begin to reshape our inner dialogue, visualization builds on that momentum by allowing us to see ourselves living out those affirming beliefs. While affirmations plant the seeds of confidence and self-worth, visualization nurtures them through mental rehearsal, helping us imagine how those beliefs look and feel in action. It's one thing to say "I am capable," and another to vividly picture yourself succeeding, staying calm under pressure, or growing through adversity. Visualization turns internal shifts into mental blueprints for real-life resilience.

Visualization is the mental practice of imagining yourself successfully navigating a challenge or achieving a desired outcome. It's a powerful resilience-building tool because the brain often doesn't distinguish between real and vividly imagined experiences. When you visualize yourself staying calm in a crisis, setting healthy boundaries, or reaching a goal, you're essentially rehearsing success in your mind. This builds confidence, reduces fear, and prepares you to act with more intention when the moment comes.

For emotional resilience, visualization can take many forms. You might picture yourself:

- Responding with calm in a difficult conversation.
- Recovering after a loss and finding peace again.
- Standing strong during uncertain times, grounded and steady.

To practice, find a quiet space, close your eyes, and mentally walk through a scene you want to prepare for. Engage all your senses—what do you see, feel, hear, or say? Let the scene play out with you at your best: resourceful, clear-headed, and centered. With repetition, this practice builds a stronger internal map for how you want to respond, making it easier to do so when real-life stress arises.

While visualization helps us mentally prepare for future strength and success, gratitude brings us back to the present—reminding us of what is already good, stable, or meaningful right now. Where visualization projects hope forward, gratitude anchors us in what we still have, even in the midst of difficulty. Together, they form a powerful balance: one fuels direction and possibility, the other fosters grounding and perspective. As we move from envisioning what's ahead to appreciating what's here, gratitude deepens our resilience by reminding us that even in struggle, there is still something worth holding onto.

Gratitude is a foundational practice for emotional resilience because it trains your mind to seek stability, meaning, and abundance—even in the face of loss or adversity. While it's never meant to dismiss pain, gratitude shifts your lens from what's missing to what's still present. That shift can make overwhelming moments feel more manageable and help the brain release dopamine and serotonin, neurochemicals that promote calm and well-being.

- Gratitude can be practiced in small, daily ways:
- Keeping a journal where you list 3 things you're grateful for.
- Writing short thank-you notes or texts to people you appreciate.

- Pausing in real time to notice beauty, safety, or comfort—a warm meal, a deep breath, a kind gesture.

In the context of emotional resilience, gratitude doesn't deny that things are hard—it simply reminds you that they're not only hard. It builds perspective, which is one of the most powerful mental muscles for bouncing back from adversity.

Emotional resilience isn't one-size-fits-all. What calms one person might overwhelm another, and what motivates you today might not serve you the same way a year from now. That's why personalizing your resilience toolbox is key to making it sustainable and effective over time. The goal isn't to master every technique—it's to identify which tools resonate with your unique personality, lifestyle, and emotional needs, and to adapt them as you evolve.

Start by noticing what already helps you reset after stress. Are you someone who needs silence and stillness, or do you feel more grounded after movement or connection? If meditation feels too passive, you might explore active mindfulness through walking or journaling. If affirmations feel forced, you could try rewriting limiting beliefs in your own words instead. Don't be afraid to experiment—test out different practices for a week or two at a time and pay attention to how they make you feel.

It also helps to create a tiered system, utilizing tools for daily use (such as a morning gratitude list or five-minute breathing exercises), tools for moments of acute stress (like grounding exercises or visualization), and tools for recovery (like therapy, nature, or creative expression). Your toolbox should be flexible and responsive, not rigid or guilt-inducing.

Finally, check in with yourself regularly. What's working? What feels stale or ineffective? Just like our bodies need varied nourishment, our minds and hearts need different types of care at different times. Personalizing your toolbox is about developing self-awareness and honoring the ways you change. Over time, this intentional approach not only strengthens your resilience but also deepens your relationship with yourself.

Resilience is built not only in theory, but also through everyday choices and personal experiences. The tools of meditation, affirmations, visualization, and gratitude may seem simple, but their power lies in how we use them during real-life challenges. The following six stories show how ordinary people applied these tools in practical, deeply personal ways to navigate stress, loss, fear, and self-doubt. Each moment of struggle became an opportunity for inner growth—proof that emotional resilience isn't about being unshakable, but about learning to steady ourselves with intention and care.

Nia's Quiet Morning

Nia had been offered a job in a new city, but the thought of uprooting her life left her feeling paralyzed. Her mind raced with "what ifs." Instead of rushing into a decision, she committed to ten minutes of guided meditation each morning. The stillness helped her untangle her anxiety from her intuition. Within a week, she was able to make the choice not from panic, but from clarity. She declined the offer, realizing she didn't actually want to leave—she just needed a change within her current life.

David's Breathing Breaks

After months of pushing through long hours and endless deadlines, David hit a wall. Exhausted and emotionally numb, he turned to a simple meditation app out of desperation. At first, he could barely sit still for two minutes. But slowly, those daily pauses gave him enough space to notice his own needs. With time, he started sleeping better, saying no more often, and showing up at work less reactive and more present.

Priya's Mirror Notes

Priya applied for her dream fellowship and was devastated when she didn't make the cut. The rejection triggered old voices in her head: "You're not smart enough. You don't belong." To counter them, she wrote daily affirmations on sticky notes and placed them on her mirror. "I am worthy even when things don't go as planned." "My value isn't defined by one outcome." Repeating those words didn't make the pain vanish, but it softened the inner critic and helped her reapply the next year, with even more clarity and confidence.

Leo's Imagined Calm

Leo needed to confront a close friend about a betrayal, but he was terrified of the conflict. His therapist suggested visualization. Each day for a week, Leo closed his eyes and pictured the conversation: breathing slowly, speaking clearly, staying steady even if things got emotional. When the time came, he didn't feel fearless, but he felt prepared. The conversation wasn't perfect, but it was honest, and Leo walked away proud of how he showed up.

Amina's Exam Strategy

Amina struggled with test anxiety, even though she knew her material well. Before her final exam, she started practicing visualization—imagining herself walking into the exam room, staying calm, reading the questions clearly, and answering with confidence. That mental rehearsal helped her nervous system stay regulated when the real moment came. For the first time, she left an exam feeling strong and grounded.

Marcus's Gratitude Shift

After a difficult breakup, Marcus felt hollow and angry. A friend encouraged him to try writing down three things he was grateful for each night, even if they were tiny—like a good meal, a sunset, or a song that moved him. At first, it felt forced. But over time, this habit started to shift his focus. He began to notice the friendships, small joys, and inner growth that were quietly carrying him forward. Gratitude didn't erase the pain— but it reminded him that life still held goodness.

Activity

"The Sensory Safety Box" – A Grounding Tool to Redirect Self-Harm Urges

This activity is designed to offer immediate comfort and grounding when self-harm urges arise. It harnesses the power of sensory engagement to reconnect you with the present moment and offer safer, soothing alternatives.

What You'll Need:

A small box, bag, or container, and a few items that appeal to your five senses. You can assemble this in advance so it's ready when needed.

What to Include (Examples):

- Touch: A smooth stone, stress ball, soft fabric, clay, or textured object
- Sight: Photos of people you love, peaceful landscapes, a comforting quote
- Smell: Lavender oil, scented lotion, herbal tea bags
- Sound: A calming playlist, wind chimes, or a note with a song suggestion
- Taste: Mints, chewing gum, or herbal tea sachets

How to Use It:

1. Pause and Breathe: When the urge to self-harm comes up, pause for a moment. Take 3 slow, deep breaths.
2. Reach for Your Box: Open the box and pick one item at a time. Focus on the texture, the scent, the feeling. Let each sense anchor you in the present.
3. Name 5 Things: If the urge feels overwhelming, name 5 things you see, 4 things you can touch, 3 things you hear, 2 things you can smell, and 1 thing you can taste. This classic grounding technique helps reset your nervous system.

4. Repeat a Reminder: Add a written note to the box that says something like, "This feeling will pass. I am allowed to ask for help. I matter."

This activity won't erase the pain, but it can offer a safe pause—a space between feeling and action, giving you time to respond with care instead of harm.

Chapter 8:
Living with Purpose and Positivity

Living with purpose and positivity means approaching each day with intention, clarity, and a hopeful mindset. In a world filled with distractions and challenges, it's easy to drift through life on autopilot, reacting instead of choosing. However, when we align our actions with our values and maintain a positive outlook, we cultivate resilience, deepen our relationships, and find greater fulfillment in even the most mundane moments. This way of living isn't about denying hardship; it's about choosing to focus on what we can control and making meaningful strides toward a life that reflects who we truly are.

Before we can truly live a life of purpose and positivity, we must first understand what drives us at our core. This means taking a closer look at the values that shape our beliefs, influence our decisions, and guide our behavior. When we align our actions with these deeply held principles, then we can begin to experience a life that feels truly meaningful. The journey starts within, by identifying what matters most to us and using that as a foundation for the way we live, work, and relate to others.

Aligning with your values to create a life of meaning is about living deliberately and authentically. At its core, this process involves identifying what truly matters to you, not what others expect, not what society dictates, but the core beliefs and principles that give your life depth and direction. These values could range from integrity, kindness, and creativity to personal growth, freedom, or service to others. When you take the time to clarify these guiding ideals, they become a steady foundation upon which you can build your decisions, relationships, and long-term goals.

Living in alignment with your values helps create a sense of inner peace and clarity. For example, if one of your core values is compassion, making time to help others, even in small ways, will bring a sense of fulfillment that far outweighs fleeting rewards. On the other hand, when your actions diverge from your values, you may experience a subtle discontent or restlessness, even if everything appears successful on the outside. That's because meaning doesn't come from achieving someone else's version of success. It comes from knowing that you're honoring who you are at your core.

This alignment also enhances your ability to make tough decisions. When faced with challenges or competing priorities, your values serve as a compass, helping you choose the path that feels most authentic and worthwhile. Over time, this consistency builds confidence and integrity, allowing others to trust and respect you, and perhaps more importantly, allowing you to trust yourself.

Ultimately, aligning with your values isn't a one-time event. It's a continuous process of reflection and recalibration, especially as you grow and evolve. But with each intentional step, you'll find yourself living with greater purpose, clarity, and a deep sense of meaning that no external achievement can replicate.

Understanding your values is a crucial first step, but living with purpose and positivity also requires regular practice and reflection. It's not enough to know what matters. You must actively create space in your life to nurture those values and keep your mindset aligned with them. By incorporating simple yet powerful exercises into your daily routine, you can stay connected to your purpose and grounded in a positive outlook, even when life becomes overwhelming or uncertain.

Discovering your purpose and staying grounded in positivity requires both self-reflection and intentional daily practice. While purpose can feel like a big, abstract concept, it often reveals itself through consistent, small steps, such as paying attention to what energizes you, what you care deeply about, and how you want to contribute to the world. Through specific exercises, you can begin to uncover these patterns and create habits that support a more positive, purpose-driven life.

One powerful exercise is journaling. As discussed before, set aside a few quiet minutes each day to write about what brought you joy, what challenged you, and what moments felt most meaningful. Over time, you may notice recurring themes or values that reflect your deeper sense of purpose. Try prompts such as, "When do I feel most alive?" or "What do I want people to remember me for?" These reflections help bring your inner motivations to the surface.

Another effective tool is a values inventory. Create a list of personal values, such as honesty, creativity, service, growth, or connection, and circle the ones that resonate with you the most. Narrow this list down to your top five and examine how well your daily life reflects these priorities. Are you honoring them in your career, relationships, and personal habits? If not, what small shifts can you make to align more closely with them?

Visualization is also a grounding technique that reinforces positivity. Take a few minutes each morning to visualize yourself living with purpose—making meaningful choices, helping others, or achieving a long-term goal. This mental practice not only boosts motivation but also sets a hopeful, focused tone for the day.

To maintain positivity, cultivate a gratitude habit. Each evening, write down three things you're grateful for, no matter how small. Gratitude shifts your attention away from what's lacking and toward what's already good in your life, fostering a mindset of abundance and resilience.

Finally, make time for mindfulness. Whether through meditation, deep breathing, or simply spending quiet time in nature, these practices help you stay present, manage stress, and reconnect with your core intentions. When you feel grounded, it becomes easier to act with clarity and purpose—even amid life's uncertainties.

By integrating these exercises into your routine, you begin to live more intentionally and with greater emotional balance. Purpose and positivity don't just happen; they're cultivated through ongoing awareness and daily commitment.

While the journey to purpose and positivity is deeply personal, hearing how others have navigated it can be both inspiring and illuminating. The following six personal stories offer powerful examples of how aligning with one's values, staying grounded in daily practices, and embracing change can lead to a more fulfilling and purposeful life.

1. Finding Purpose Through Service

Maria, a nurse in her mid-30s, often felt drained by the demands of her job. Until a moment of clarity changed everything. One evening, after helping a young patient through a difficult diagnosis, the patient's mother hugged Maria and said, "You made us feel human in all this." That moment helped Maria realize her purpose wasn't just clinical care, it was compassion. She began journaling each night about meaningful patient interactions, which reconnected her to her core value: empathy. This renewed sense of purpose not only re-energized her work but also deepened her relationships at home.

2. Choosing Authenticity Over Approval

Devin was a graphic designer, and he spent years chasing promotions and recognition at a firm where his creative freedom was limited. He often felt conflicted but didn't want to "rock the boat." During a values inventory exercise in a self-development workshop, he realized his top values were creativity, freedom, and integrity. These weren't reflected in his daily work. Encouraged by this insight, Devin slowly built a freelance business on the side and eventually made the leap. Though the transition was scary, aligning his work with his values brought him greater satisfaction, and clients who truly appreciated his unique voice.

3. Turning Loss into Meaning

After losing her father unexpectedly, Samira felt lost and directionless. During her grieving process, she began writing letters to her father, reflecting on the lessons he taught her. Over time, she noticed a recurring theme: his relentless optimism and kindness to everyone he met. Inspired by his example, Samira started volunteering at a local food bank, something her father had always wanted to do. Through service and gratitude journaling, she found peace and a renewed sense of purpose, honoring his memory by embodying the values he lived by.

4. From Burnout to Balance

Eli was a high-achieving software engineer who worked long hours and rarely disconnected. When stress led to burnout and a health scare, he took a step back to re-evaluate his priorities. Through daily mindfulness meditation and journaling, Eli discovered he valued balance, well-being, and curiosity more than recognition. He began setting boundaries at work, saying no more often, and exploring creative hobbies like painting and hiking. Not only did his health improve, but his focus and happiness also improved. His purpose became clear: to live a life that supports both ambition and peace.

5. Reconnecting with Joy

Nina, a retired teacher, struggled with identity loss after stepping away from the classroom. She felt untethered, unsure of her role in the world. At the suggestion of a friend, she began a simple gratitude practice—writing down three things she was thankful for each night. Over time, she began noticing the joy in small things: her garden, weekly phone calls with former students, the laughter of her grandchildren. This daily habit helped Nina reconnect with her purpose: nurturing growth, whether in children or in her own backyard.

6. Living Boldly Through Change

After moving to a new city for a job, Andre struggled with loneliness and self-doubt. To stay grounded, he revisited a personal visualization exercise from a life coach he once worked with. Each morning, he envisioned himself confident, connected, and living in alignment with his values—adventure, connection, and honesty. He joined local hiking groups, started a blog about navigating change, and slowly built a new circle of friends. By acting from his values instead of fear, Andre transformed uncertainty into a season of deep personal growth and discovery.

As we arrive at the final chapter of this journey, take a moment to pause—truly pause—and honor how far you've come. This book wasn't just a collection of thoughts and exercises; it was a heartfelt guide meant to reconnect you with something deeper: your own inner compass.

We began by acknowledging that life is full of emotional storms—times of grief, anger, confusion, and loss. But rather than being swept away by them, you've learned how to stand still, reflect, and move forward with grace. Through the RPNB method—Reflect, Pause, Navigate, and Balance—you now have a framework that transforms chaos into clarity, reaction into response, and confusion into conscious living.

You explored how aligning with your values gives your life meaning, how identifying what matters most to you can serve as a guiding star when the way ahead feels uncertain. You discovered the importance of reflection, not just as a tool for insight but as a daily practice for emotional freedom and healing.

You embraced the pause—a small moment with big power. You learned to sit still when emotions flare, to breathe before reacting, and to let that space create calm rather than conflict.

You practiced how to navigate life's messiness, not with perfection, but with purpose. You saw how choosing intentional responses over impulsive reactions allows you to move through even the most difficult moments with integrity.

And most importantly, you found your balance. Through self-care, healthy routines, and meaningful boundaries, you created the scaffolding for a more grounded, peaceful, and resilient life.

Along the way, you met stories of others. Some may say that their journeys were conveniently changed at a random moment, but that's the whole point. These stories were selected because they are random. So that you, the reader, can understand that change doesn't come with a grand gesture or a moment, it's just a sudden realization you can have on a random Wednesday sitting with your friend/coworker/alone.

You've explored journaling, affirmations, visualizations, and grounding techniques. You've written letters to sadness, embraced your inner dialogue, and learned how to give yourself grace. These tools are now yours. They are your anchors in rough seas and your torch in the dark.

So, where do you go from here?

You keep going. One mindful step at a time. You revisit these pages whenever you need a reminder. You let your growth unfold gently, layer by layer. You share what you've learned with others who are still searching for their way. And you return to your compass—your true self—again and again.

You are no longer lost. You've simply found your way back to yourself.

Final Activity

The Compass Letter

Purpose:

To solidify your growth by writing a letter to your future self, anchored in the wisdom, clarity, and strength you've gained throughout this journey.

Instructions:

1. **Find a Quiet Space**
2. Sit somewhere peaceful, where you feel calm and undistracted. Bring your journal or a blank piece of paper. Take a few deep breaths to ground yourself in the present moment.
3. **Begin the Letter to Your Future Self**
   Imagine you're writing to yourself six months or even a year from now. A version of you who might be facing new challenges, carrying self-doubt, or simply needing a gentle reminder of their strength.

Start with:

"Dear Me, I want you to remember..."

Then write freely. Let your words flow. Consider including:

- What you've learned about yourself through this journey
- Which values matter most to you now and why
- What you hope you'll continue to do when things feel hard
- What your emotional compass looks like when you're aligned

4. **Include Encouragement and Affirmation**

   Speak kindly. Be your own cheerleader. Write the words you know you'll need to hear—because who better to guide you than the version of you who's walked through the storm and found peace?

5. **Seal or Save It**

   Once you finish, fold the letter and tuck it somewhere safe. Or set a reminder to reread it in a few months. Let it become a message in a bottle—from your present self to your future self.

6. **End with Intention**

   At the bottom of your letter, write the affirmation that encapsulates everything you now believe, everything you are stepping into:

"Your compass is always within you—trust it, and navigate life with confidence."

Let this be your final reflection—a promise to yourself that you will continue to move forward with clarity, strength, and purpose.

A Note from the Author

Dear Reader,

If you're reading this, you've made it to the end, and that's something truly worth celebrating.

You didn't just finish a book; you showed up for yourself. You explored difficult emotions, leaned into self-reflection, and embraced tools that many shy away from. That takes courage. That takes heart.

Thank you for letting me be a small part of your journey. I'm cheering you on, always.

With warmth and admiration,

Valerie Jones